NAME THAT ANIMAL

By Noah Tye

Illustrations by Iryna Novytska

NAME THAT ANIMAL

iUniverse books may be ordered through booksellers or by contacting:

iUniverse
1663 Liberty Drive
Bloomington, IN 47403
www.iuniverse.com
1-800-Authors (1-800-288-4677)

ISBN: 978-1-5320-5732-8 (sc)
ISBN: 978-1-5320-5733-5 (e)
ISBN: 978-1-5320-7310-6 (hc)

Library of Congress Control Number: 2018910954

Print information available on the last page.

iUniverse rev. date: 04/15/2019

Acknowledgements

There are many people to acknowledge for the creation of this book.

I would like to thank my mother, Mona, for her love and support. She also helped in giving her input about developmentally appropriate material. Thank you for continuing to give me unconditional love and support.
Thank you to the entire Tye/Flagler family for positive encouragement.

Thank you to the Schwartz/Salowitz family: Hanna, Doc, Noah, Chaya and Coby. You have given helpful feedback on content and design.

Thank you to Eli Abramowitz, Marissa Cohen, Ethan King, Briana Lavintman, Leivik Fogelman, Shmulik Fogelman and the Fogelman family, Mendel Levin, Matis Nitzlich, Shari Perelmuter, Daniel Raskin, Lana Rogoff, Shloma Solomon, and Benjamin Zand for advice on illustrations and your encouragement.

I would also like to thank Eric Golub for giving me advice on book format, supplying resources, time, and energy.

Thank you to Dr. Reus Chaya Hersh, Mrs. Sarah Fishman and Dr. Paul Black for providing excellent consultation.

Thanks to all my friends and family for providing inspiration.

A special thanks to Iryna Novytska for your beautiful illustrations. You made this book look amazing.

Thank you to Michaela Lazuka for taking my author photo.

A

IS FOR

ALLIGATOR

B
IS FOR
BEAR

C
IS FOR
CAMEL

D
IS FOR
DOG

E
IS FOR
ELEPHANT

F
IS FOR
FROG

G

IS FOR

GOAT

H
IS FOR
HORSE

I
IS FOR
IGUANA

J

IS FOR

JELLYFISH

IS FOR
KANGAROO

M
IS FOR
MONKEY

N
IS FOR
NEWT

O
IS FOR
OWL

P

IS FOR

PIG

IS FOR
QUAIL

R
IS FOR
RAM

S

IS FOR

SHEEP

T
IS FOR
TIGER

U

IS FOR

URCHIN

V
IS FOR
VULTURE

W
IS FOR
WOLF

X
IS FOR
X-RAY FISH

Y
IS FOR
YAK

Z
IS FOR
ZEBRA

Printed in the United States
By Bookmasters